Vegetarian

Published originally in Italian as *Vegetariana*
© 2005 Food Editore srl
Via Bordoni, 8 - 20124 MILAN, ITALY
Via Mazzini, 6 - 43100 PARMA, ITALY

English Translation
Traduzioni Culinarie

Photographs
Alberto Rossi and Davide Di Prato

Recipes
Simone Rugiati and Licia Cagnoni

Thanks to
I Love My House (Barazzoni, Parma)

This 2008 edition printed exclusively for Barnes & Noble, Inc.,
by Food Editore srl.

ISBN-13: 978-1-4351-0623-9

Printed and bound in China
10 9 8 7 6 5 4 3 2 1

Vegetarian

Great Recipes from the Chefs of Food Editore

FOOD
EDITORE

Parma, Milan

Contents

Basic Techniques

VEGETARIAN FOOD AND GREEN COOKING

A vegetarian diet isn't boring or nutritionally deficient, as some might imagine. Instead it is a balanced, healthy, and rational way of eating. Vegetarian cuisine is no longer a niche, the choice of a small minority, but an important part of mainstream food culture. Consumers are more interested than ever in buying vegetables and vegetarian products.

Vegetables are an important source of vitamins and minerals, and can also help prevent diseases. When we were children, our parents may have chased us around the table insisting we force down at least a tiny portion of vegetables, but as adults we can learn to appreciate and enjoy the flavors offered by a vast range of produce.

THE NUTRITIONAL IMPORTANCE OF VEGETABLES

Greens, fruits, and grains are known to be an important part of a healthy, balanced diet. Eating these foods regularly helps to prevent numerous health problems. According to nutritionists and governments, our body's ideal "dose" of fruits and vegetables is about five servings per day. For breakfast, lunch, dinner, and snacks, health professionals recommend a daily diet rich in fruits and vegetables. Why are fruits and vegetables so important? Because they are packed with important nutrients. Not only are they low in fat, but fruits and vegetables contain a modest amount of simple sugars and proteins. Moreover, they are an important source of vitamins, minerals, and dietary fiber.

Vitamins

Vitamins present in edible vegetables can be divided into two groups: fat-soluble, such as vitamins A, D, and E; water-soluble, such as vitamin C; and the various vitamins in the B group. Retinol, the animal form of **vitamin A**, has important properties that strengthen sight and help to maintain healthy skin; it can also aid fertility, together with vitamin E. However, beta carotene, which is transformed by the human organism into vitamin A, is present in some vegetables. Beta carotene is found in carrots (and named after them), dark green leafy vegetables, and some fruits, including papaya and mango. **Vitamin E** is often found in grains. In fact, wheat-germ oil is one of the most important sources of vitamin E. One of the many good benefits of eating whole-wheat grains is their high vitamin E content. The vitamin is also present in asparagus, avocados, almonds, and walnuts. **B vitamins** are most commonly found in such whole-grain cereals as wheat germ, in nuts (pine nuts, peanuts, walnuts, and pistachios), and in legumes. The B vitamins are needed to transform carbohydrates, fat, and protein into usable energy; they also help to regenerate tissue in the human body. A lack of these vitamins can have serious consequences, from weak muscles to nervous system disorders. **Vitamin K** helps bone development and is found in green leafy vegetables such as spinach, chard, and cabbage. **Vitamin C,** or ascorbic acid, is present in nearly all fruits and vegetables, particularly citrus fruits, tomatoes, wild berries, and broccoli. It is an important antioxidant that protects the body from free radicals, which medical researchers believe are linked to the formation of cancer cells and are also a cause of aging.

Fresh vegetables contain the highest levels of vitamins and minerals. It is important to eat vegetables that are freshly picked and briefly cooked. We suggest using organic produce when possible, as eating fruits and vegetables

that have been heavily treated with herbicides and pesticides may cause more damage than the benefits that the foods may offer.

Minerals

These components, present in varying quantities in vegetables, help to regulate many of the functions of the human organism. Potassium, calcium, phosphorus, magnesium, manganese, zinc, copper, iron, and selenium are among the most important minerals.

Dietary Fiber

Dietary fiber is indigestible vegetable matter and plays an important role in digestion. Foods rich in dietary fiber can be denser and require more chewing, stimulating saliva emissions and the initial enzymes that aid in digestion and the absorption of nutrients. Part of the dietary fiber acts as "food" for intestinal bacteria, allowing the production of some vitamins (B and K). Eating fiber-rich foods also results in a sense of fullness, limiting overeating and unnecessary snacking.

VEGANS, VEGETARIANS, GRANIVORES, ETC.

A vegetarian diet excludes fish, poultry, and meat (the direct consumption of animals), but allows for the use of animal products such as milk, eggs, and their derivatives.

Vegetarians can be divided into three groups: those who consume both egg and milk products, those who will not consume egg products, and those who will not consume milk products.

There are other more restrictive dietary regimens, which are often linked to moral questions regarding the consumption of animals and animal-derived products. Vegans, for example, do not eat meat, poultry, or fish, and exclude any products derived from animals, including milk, eggs, or honey.

The word vegetarian derives from the Latin *vegetus*, which means healthy, and the term vegan indicates one who eats only vegetables (from the Latin *vegetabilis*). From a health perspective, a vegan diet is more difficult to follow without significant nutritional and scientific knowledge. Certain dietary regimens are selective about the provenance of foods and exclude some vegetables. Granivores eat only seeds and grains, while fruitarians eat only fruit. A growing number of people also choose to

eat only raw foods. Such extreme dietary regimens can cause health risks because of imbalances of the macronutrients (proteins, fats, and sugars) necessary to the human organism.

Why become vegetarian or vegan? There are many reasons. For some it is a lifestyle choice based on the health benefits, while for others it is a moral, ethical, or environmental decision.

VEGETABLES, GRAINS, AND MEAT SUBSTITUTES

We have seen how vegetables, fruits, and grains make up an important part of our diet, as they contain micro- and macronutrients, dietary fiber, and beneficial vitamins and minerals. However, our aim is not to convert readers to vegetarianism, but to promote the concept that cooking without meat is not only healthy but can also be delicious and creative, and that fruits and vegetables can be the basis for the whole meal, not just a side dish.

Vegetable proteins are a delicious and healthy substitute for the traditional steak or chop, and grains, a primary nutrient for humans, are the main ingredient in many hearty first-course dishes and desserts.

The recipes in this book offer tantalizing suggestions on how to prepare the fruits of the earth (vegetables, beans, and grains) in many diverse ways, all without using meat or fish.

Seasonal Vegetables

In this book, you can learn how to prepare appetizing main dishes with seasonal vegetables.

We believe in eating only fruits and vegetables that are in season.

If seasonal fruits and vegetables are no longer available to consumers, and harvests are no longer dependent on the seasons thanks to greenhouse cultivation, hormones, hybrids, and genetically modified foods, then consumers have lost touch with the seasons themselves. Globalization and advances in transportation have made it possible to find a wide variety of fruits and vegetables year-round.

As convenient as it may be, such produce is often tasteless and poorer in nutrients than its seasonal counterpart. Better to trust a greengrocer or a market gardener and buy only seasonal produce, which is often also cheaper.

METHODS FOR COOKING VEGETABLES

For best results use the freshest possible organic vegetables. Vegetables should be carefully washed and left to drip dry. Vegetables lose their important nutrients as they are cooked so it is best to eat them raw whenever possible. When cooking them, use techniques that allow the vegetables to cook quickly and delicately. When boiling, water should never be salted before the vegetable is immersed, but just after. Alternatively, vegetables may be salted before adding them to the boiling water. The cooking water may be reused as a soup base or broth. Below is a list of common techniques that are used in various parts of the world for cooking vegetables.

Baking/roasting: Any vegetable can be baked or roasted, and certain vegetables can be blanched before baking. Roasting is a simple technique in which vegetables are baked—uncovered—until golden brown. It is especially good for root vegetables and requires little added fat. Baking is commonly used for dishes such as gratins, where vegetables are covered with cheese or béchamel and baked until a golden crust forms over the top.

Boiling: This option requires a large pot in which the vegetables to be cooked have plenty of space. Vegetables may be cooked starting from cold water, or immersed directly in boiling water, depending on the type. Leafy greens should be cooked uncovered, while potatoes should be immersed in cold water that is then brought to a boil. In some cases, as with spinach, the vegetables may be cooked without using any water because they, themselves, release the water necessary for cooking. Dry beans and legumes should first be soaked for at least 12 hours in cold water before boiling in fresh water.

Grilling: Vegetables to be grilled should be thickly sliced and seasoned with extra-virgin olive oil, salt, pepper, and mixed herbs before grilling. If using a barbecue, make sure that the coals are white and there are no flames. A grill pan is a quick and convenient solution for grilling vegetables indoors.

Steaming: This is the cooking method that best maintains vegetables' important nutrients. Vegetables are placed in a metal or bamboo basket over boiling water. They never come in contact with the cooking water, thus retaining important vitamins and minerals.

SEITAN, TOFU, AND TEMPEH

Vegetarian and vegan recipes make frequent use of seitan, tofu, and tempeh, but what are they? They are in fact vegetable-derived foods, originally from Asia, that contain a high level of vegetable protein. This makes them good substitutes for meat, poultry, fish, and eggs in a non-animal-based diet. Furthermore, they are delicious and thus can play a healthy and tasty role in every kitchen.

Tofu and tempeh are both made from soy, a versatile legume that is high in proteins and unsaturated fats. Other soy-based products include milk, miso (fermented soybean paste or powder), tamari, shoyu (soy sauce), and lecithin.

is made from wheat gluten and is an ingredient in vegetarian and macrobiotic cooking. The wheat gluten is mixed together with water and then cooked for a few hours. Seitan can also be made with wheat bran rinsed and kneaded under cold running water several times and then worked to form a smooth and elastic mass made up of gluten and a small amount of residual starches, fats, and minerals. This second method, while economical, isn't advised as it is very labor intensive. Seitan may be purchased already made in health and natural-food stores. It is usually flavored and prepared together with other natural ingredients. A high-protein food low in fat and carbohydrates, it is filling, has a neutral flavor, and pairs well with vegetable-based sauces. The proteins in seitan are not complete, so it is best to prepare it with legumes when making main dishes.

Tempeh is a soy-based protein, used a lot in Indonesia. The fungus *Rhizopus oligosporus* is added to cooked yellow soybeans. This fungus causes the soy to ferment, creating tempeh, which contains almost 20% protein and all of the essential amino acids, as well as vitamin B12.

Tofu, also known as bean curd, is a food of Chinese origin made from soy milk, which is coagulated with nigari (magnesium chlorate extracted from sea water)—or, more commonly, with lemon juice—and pressed into blocks. It is a high-protein food that is extremely easy to digest. Low in fat and cholesterol-free, it has a neutral taste that makes it well-suited to a range of different uses in the kitchen; it can be eaten raw, stir-fried, included in soup, or deep-fried, to name a few.

CEREALS AND GRAINS

Although whole grains are underused in modern cuisine, especially in developed countries, they are the principal food source for the majority of people in the world. Farro (emmer wheat), buckwheat, and rye are often only part of specific diets, and do not play a large role in regular daily meals. More exotic cereals and grains, such as South American quinoa, are used even less frequently, but are slowly gaining popularity. Only wheat, corn, and rice, in their most refined forms, are used regularly on a large-scale basis. When refined, cereals and grains lose many of their nutrients. Some of these little-known cereals and grains can be ground and used for pasta or bread, but for the most part, these great food resources are neglected by the northern hemisphere. Whole grains can be found in various forms including sprouts, flakes, and flours. Their nutritional value depends greatly on the way they have been refined. The germ contains a particularly large part of the energy-giving nutrients in cereals and grains. Cereals play an important part in traditional Chinese medicine, with each cereal linked to a specific body part. Oats, for example, are considered an important energy source for the lungs, while rye helps liver. Rice and corn are thought to be important for the correct functioning of the pancreas and spleen.

Pasta, Rice, and Grains

These creative first courses offer
a healthy way to satisfy the appetite
without sacrificing taste.

Rigatoni with Chickpeas and Seaweed

Serves 4

½ cup (3½ ounces) dried chickpeas, soaked overnight
2 bay leaves
2 tablespoons arame seaweed
extra-virgin olive oil
1 garlic clove
soy sauce
salt
12 ounces whole-wheat rigatoni

Preparation time 15 minutes
Cooking time 1 hour 15 minutes
Level easy

Boil the chickpeas with the bay leaves in a pressure cooker for 50 minutes. Soak the seaweed in cold water for 10 minutes, then drain and chop.

Heat the olive oil in a frying pan and add the garlic. Let brown, then add the seaweed. Add the chickpeas and soy sauce to taste, and sauté briefly.

Cook the rigatoni in a pot of salted boiling water until al dente. Drain and transfer to the pan with the sauce. Sauté for 1 minute and serve immediately.

Farro Crêpes with Peas

Serves 4

Crêpes
¾ cup plus 1 tablespoon (3½ ounces) farro (emmer wheat) flour
¾ cup plus 1 tablespoon (3½ ounces) all-purpose flour
2 cups milk
2 eggs
salt and white pepper
extra-virgin olive oil

Filling
2 tablespoons extra-virgin olive oil
1 shallot, minced
2⅓ cups (12½ ounces) new peas
½ cup vegetable broth
2 tablespoons soy cream

Garnish
2 ounces Mimolette cheese (or other aged cow's-milk cheese), shaved

Preparation time 25 minutes
Cooking time 30 minutes
Level medium

Preheat the oven to 400°F.

Sift the two flours into a mixing bowl. Gradually whisk in the milk and eggs. Season with salt and pepper and let rest for 20 minutes. Strain the batter to remove any lumps.

Heat the olive oil in a frying pan, sauté the shallot and peas, and cover with broth. Let cook over low heat for 15 minutes. Remove from heat and puree with the cream. The mixture should be quite thick.

Heat a crêpe pan (or small nonstick frying pan) and lightly coat with olive oil. Pour 1 small ladleful of batter into the pan and quickly spread it into a very thin layer. Flip and cook for 1 minute. Remove from heat. Repeat until batter is finished. Let the crêpes cool.

Spread pea puree on each crêpe and roll up. Place the crêpes in a baking dish and cover with aluminum foil. Bake for 5 minutes. Remove from heat, slice, and sprinkle with cheese shavings.

Farro Tagliatelle with Truffle Cream

Serves 4

1 tablespoon extra-virgin olive oil
½ white onion, minced
½ teaspoon grated fresh ginger
1 black truffle, shaved
1 cup soy cream
salt and pepper
11 ounces farro tagliatelle (or fettuccine)
1 handful of pine nuts

Preparation time 10 minutes
Cooking time 20 minutes
Level easy

Heat the olive oil in a frying pan and add the onion. Sauté briefly and add 1 tablespoon of water. Add the ginger and truffle. Pour in the soy cream and reduce over low heat. Season with salt and pepper.

Cook the pasta in a large pot of salted boiling water until al dente. Drain and transfer to the sauce. Sauté for 1 minute to coat with sauce. Top with pine nuts and serve immediately.

Buckwheat Maltagliati with Fresh Tomatoes

Serves 4

Maltagliati
1²/₃ cups (7 ounces) all-purpose flour
1²/₃ cups (7 ounces) buckwheat flour
pinch of salt

Sauce
2 ripe tomatoes
2 tablespoons extra-virgin olive oil
1 garlic clove
2 teaspoons dried thyme leaves
salt

Garnish
parsley, chopped
extra-virgin olive oil

Preparation time 25 minutes
Cooking time 25 minutes
Level easy

Sift the two flours and salt onto a work surface and add enough warm water to form a smooth dough. Knead vigorously for 10 minutes until the dough is firm. Let rest for 30 minutes.

Meanwhile, blanch, drain, peel, and dice the tomatoes.

Heat the olive oil in a frying pan and add the garlic clove. When the garlic begins to brown, remove it and add the tomatoes and thyme leaves. Season with salt. Simmer for 10 minutes and remove from heat.

Roll out the dough into thin sheets. Cut the sheets into irregular rectangles (maltagliati). Cook the maltagliati in a large pot of salted boiling water for 5 minutes. Drain the pasta and top with the tomato sauce. Serve hot with chopped parsley and a drizzle of olive oil.

Penne with Zucchini and Pesto

Serves 4

Pasta
1 tablespoon extra-virgin olive oil
1 onion, thinly sliced
2 zucchini, sliced
salt
6 squash blossoms, julienned
7 ounces penne pasta

Pesto
1 bunch of basil, stemmed
2 tablespoons pine nuts
½ teaspoon barley miso
3 tablespoons extra-virgin olive oil

Preparation time 20 minutes
Cooking time 20 minutes
Level easy

BASIL
Basil is an aromatic herb originally from India. The Greek name for basil, *basilikón*, means regal herb, suggesting that at one time it may have been scarce. Basil should always be used fresh and should be torn by hand, never chopped with a knife, as contact with metal may alter its taste.

Heat 1 tablespoon olive oil in a frying pan. Add the onion and 2 tablespoons of water and cook until soft. Add the zucchini, season with salt, and cook for 10 to 15 minutes. Add the squash blossoms and remove from heat.

Make the pesto: Blend the basil, pine nuts, miso, and olive oil in a food processor or use a mortar and pestle.

Cook the pasta in a large pot of salted boiling water until al dente. Drain, reserving 2 tablespoons of cooking water, and add to the zucchini mixture with the cooking water. Sauté for a few minutes. Add the pesto and toss to coat. Serve immediately.

Shells with Mushrooms and Squash Blossoms

Serves 4

3 tablespoons extra-virgin olive oil
2 shallots, minced
1 large fresh porcini mushroom, chopped
1⅓ cups (3½ ounces) chopped white mushrooms
salt and pepper
8 squash blossoms, minced
½ cup vegetable broth
1 tablespoon soy cream
1 teaspoon cornstarch
11 ounces large pasta shells

Preparation time 20 minutes
Cooking time 30 minutes
Level easy

Heat 2 tablespoons olive oil in a frying pan and add half of the minced shallots. Sauté over low heat and then add the mushrooms. Season with salt and pepper and sauté for 10 minutes.

Meanwhile, heat the remaining olive oil in a small saucepan and add the remaining minced shallot. When the shallot is soft, add the squash blossoms. Pour the broth in and cook for 5 minutes. Add the cream and whisk in cornstarch to thicken the sauce.

Cook the pasta shells in a large pot of salted boiling water until al dente. Drain and fill with the mushrooms. Serve on top of the squash blossom sauce.

Penne with Roasted Pepper Sauce and Almonds

Serves 4

½ yellow bell pepper
½ red bell pepper
3 tablespoons extra-virgin olive oil
1 onion, diced
¾ cup vegetable broth
salt and pepper
2 tablespoons oat cream
12 ounces farro (emmer wheat) penne
2 tablespoons sliced or slivered almonds

Preparation time 10 minutes
Cooking time 30 minutes
Level easy

Roast the peppers over an open flame, either under the broiler or in the oven, until the skin begins to blacken. Place the peppers in a plastic bag, close, and let sit for 10 to 15 minutes to steam. Remove, peel, seed, and cut into strips.

Heat the olive oil in a frying pan and add the onion. Sauté briefly, then add the roasted peppers and broth. Cover and cook for 15 minutes over low heat. Season with salt and pepper to taste, then puree with the oat cream in a blender or food processor.

Cook the penne in a large pot of salted boiling water until al dente. Meanwhile, toast the almonds in a nonstick frying pan over low heat. Drain the penne and toss together with the roasted pepper sauce. Top with the toasted almonds.

Squash Tortelli

Serves 4

Filling
2 tablespoons extra-virgin olive oil
1 yellow onion, diced
14 ounces Kabocha or other green-skinned winter squash, diced
1 thyme sprig
salt and pepper
2 amaretto cookies

Dough
2¾ cups (12½ ounces) all-purpose flour
1 egg
3 egg yolks
salt

Sauce
2 tablespoons butter
1 onion, minced
6 sage leaves

Garnish
aged pecorino cheese, grated

Preparation time 1 hour
Cooking time 25 minutes
Level medium

Heat the olive oil in a frying pan with the onion for the filling. Add 1 tablespoon of water and cook for 5 minutes over low heat. Add the squash and thyme and cook for 12 minutes. Season with salt and pepper and remove from heat. Puree the squash with the amaretto cookies until smooth.

Mound the flour on a work surface and make a well in the center. Add the egg, egg yolks, and a pinch of salt. Quickly mix together to form a smooth dough. Cover with a clean kitchen towel and let rest for 10 minutes.

Roll out the pasta dough into thin sheets. Place spoonfuls of the squash puree at intervals of 2 inches along the dough. Cover with a second sheet of dough and press down around the filling to seal. Cut out tortelli using a rolling serrated pasta cutter. Heat the butter for the sauce in a frying pan and add the onion and sage leaves. Sauté until the butter begins to brown and smell nutty.

Cook the tortelli in a large pot of salted boiling water until they rise to the surface. Drain with a slotted spoon and transfer to the butter and sage sauce. Toss the tortelli in the pan to coat. Sprinkle with aged pecorino cheese.

Buckwheat Tagliatelle with Porcini

Serves 4

3 tablespoons extra-virgin olive oil
1 garlic clove, minced
½ dried red chili pepper, minced
3 to 4 fresh porcini mushrooms, thinly sliced
salt
12 ounces buckwheat tagliatelle or fettuccine
parsley, chopped
thyme, chopped
2 tablespoons soy cream

Preparation time 15 minutes
Cooking time 20 minutes
Level easy

Heat the olive oil in a frying pan and add the garlic and chili pepper. Sauté until the garlic begins to turn color, then add the mushrooms. Sauté the mixture for 10 minutes, sprinkling with parsley and thyme.

Cook the pasta in a large pot of salted boiling water until al dente.

Meanwhile add the cream and one ladleful of the pasta cooking water to the sauce, and cook down until thick. When the pasta is ready, drain, transfer to the pan with the sauce, and toss to coat. Serve immediately.

Variation For a rich version, add shaved truffles to this pasta dish.

Farro Crêpes with Asparagus

Serves 4

Crêpes
1 ½ cups (5 ounces) farro (emmer wheat) flour
6 ½ tablespoons all-purpose flour
2 tablespoons soy cream
salt
1 ¾ cups soy milk
extra-virgin olive oil

Filling
2 tablespoons extra-virgin olive oil
1 shallot, minced
15 asparagus spears (about 10 ½ ounces), trimmed and chopped
salt and pepper
3 tablespoons corn oil
4 tablespoons all-purpose flour
1 cup soy milk
ground nutmeg

Topping
⅔ cup soy cream
2 tablespoons breadcrumbs

Preparation time 35 minutes
Cooking time 30 minutes
Level medium

Preheat the oven to 400°F. Mix the two flours for the crêpes in a bowl. Add the soy cream and salt and whisk in the soy milk. Let the batter rest for 20 minutes. Heat the olive oil for the filling in a saucepan and add the shallot. Cook until soft, then add the asparagus. Season with salt and add ½ cup water. Simmer for 15 minutes over low heat. Puree the mixture and set aside.

Heat the corn oil in a saucepan and add the flour. Cook the flour for a few minutes over low heat and then whisk in the soy milk. Cook for 10 minutes, stirring constantly. Season with salt and nutmeg to taste. Add to the asparagus puree.

Heat a crêpe pan (8-inches in diameter) or nonstick frying pan of the same size. Coat lightly with olive oil. Pour 1 small ladleful of batter into the pan and quickly spread it into a very thin layer. Cook for 1 minute, flip, and cook for 1 more minute. Remove from heat. Repeat until batter is finished.

Fill each crêpe with the asparagus cream and fold into quarters. Place the crêpes in a baking dish, drizzle with soy cream, and sprinkle with breadcrumbs. Bake for 10 minutes.

Millet Timbales with Bell Peppers and Zucchini

Serves 4

4 tablespoons extra-virgin olive oil
½ yellow onion, finely diced
1 cup (7 ounces) millet
vegetable broth
2 zucchini
½ red bell pepper, seeded and diced
½ yellow bell pepper, seeded and diced
salt and pepper
4 mint leaves, minced

Preparation time 20 minutes
Cooking time 25 minutes
Level easy

Sauté the onion in 2 tablespoons of olive oil for a few minutes. Add a little water and cook until the onion is soft. Add the millet and cover with broth. Cover the pot and cook for 15 minutes. Remove from the heat and set aside.

Trim the zucchini and slice lengthwise into quarters. Remove the seedy center and dice the rest. Heat the remaining olive oil in a non-stick frying pan and sauté the peppers for 4 minutes. Add the zucchini and sauté until tender. Season to taste with salt and pepper and add the cooked millet. Add the mint leaves and stir to combine all of the ingredients. Fill 4 molds with the millet mixture, then unmold them onto serving plates.

Variation Cook the millet together with 2¾ cups (14 ounces) diced pumpkin. When the cooked mixture has cooled, transfer it to a baking dish and pour over cup soy cream and ½ cup (2 ounce) chopped walnuts. Bake for 15 minutes at 300°F.

Orecchiette with Broccoli and Fonduta Sauce

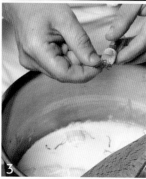

Serves 4

½ head broccoli, cut into small florets
3 tablespoons extra-virgin olive oil
1 garlic clove, smashed
salt and pepper
5½ ounces Taleggio cheese, cut into matchsticks
⅓ cup heavy cream
1 pinch dried saffron
12 ounces orecchiette
2 tablespoons grated Parmesan cheese

Preparation time 10 minutes
Cooking time 25 minutes
Level easy

Blanch the broccoli in a large pot of lightly salted boiling water. Drain with a slotted spoon and reserve the cooking water.

Heat the olive oil in a frying pan and add the garlic clove. Sauté briefly, then add the broccoli (photo 1) and cook for 10 minutes over medium heat. Season with salt and pepper to taste.

Melt the Taleggio and cream in a saucepan (photo 2) and add the saffron (photo 3). Once the mixture has melted into a smooth sauce, pour a little over the broccoli.

Bring the broccoli cooking water back to a boil and cook the orecchiette until al dente. Drain and transfer the pasta to the pan with the broccoli. Sauté for a few minutes over high heat. Add the remaining sauce and remove from heat. Toss to coat the pasta with sauce and sprinkle with Parmesan cheese. Serve immediately.

Farro Rigatoni with Cauliflower

Serves 4

1 medium cauliflower (about 1 pound), cut into small florets
salt
11 ounces farro (emmer wheat) pasta
2 tablespoons extra-virgin olive oil
2 garlic cloves, thinly sliced
1 pinch dried red chili pepper flakes
1 tablespoon minced parsley
2 tablespoons gomasio (see note below)

Preparation time 10 minutes
Cooking time 15 minutes
Level easy

Bring 2 quarts water to a boil. Add the cauliflower, then salt and boil for 5 minutes. Add the pasta and cook until al dente.

Meanwhile, heat the olive oil in a frying pan and add the garlic and a pinch of chili pepper flakes. Sauté until the garlic browns. Strain the oil.

Drain the pasta and cauliflower and drizzle with the garlic-chili oil. Add the parsley and gomasio. Mix and serve immediately.

Note Gomasio is a Japanese seasoning, which can be made at home by toasting 5 tablespoons of sesame seeds in a nonstick pan over medium-high heat for 2 to 3 minutes. Lower the heat and continue toasting until the seeds crumble easily between the fingertips. Transfer to a mortar and mash the seeds with ½ teaspoon salt to form a smooth paste.

Rice with Pumpkin and Potatoes

Serves 4

1 tablespoon extra-virgin olive oil
½ white onion, diced
2 cups vegetable broth
¼ pumpkin, peeled, seeded, and diced
2 yellow-fleshed potatoes, peeled and diced
1 celery stalk, julienned
7 asparagus spears, trimmed and julienned
1⅓ cups parboiled long-grain and wild rice mix
1 teaspoon curry powder

Preparation time 25 minutes
Cooking time 25 minutes
Level easy

Heat the olive oil and sauté the onion with a little vegetable broth. Add the pumpkin and potatoes and cook for 5 minutes, then add the celery and asparagus and cook over low heat for 3 to 4 minutes.

Cook the rice in vegetable broth for 15 minutes. Let sit for 5 minutes. Add the curry to the vegetables and stir in the rice. Sauté over high heat and serve hot.

Variation For another original rice and pumpkin dish, take one pound of sliced pumpkin and roast in the oven. Dress with lemon juice and grated horseradish, then sauté briefly with cooked rice. Serve hot.

Chard and Ricotta Gnocchi

Serves 6

Gnocchi
1 ½ pounds Swiss chard
14 ounces ricotta
4 eggs
2 ⅓ cups plus 1 tablespoon (10 ½ ounces) all-purpose flour
nutmeg, grated
salt

Sauce
melted butter
4 tablespoons grated Parmesan cheese

Preparation time 30 minutes
Cooking time 20 minutes
Level easy

Blanch the Swiss chard in boiling water until tender. Drain, trim off white ribs, and finely slice the green leaves.

Place the ricotta in a bowl and add the chard, eggs, flour, and a grating of nutmeg. Stir until thoroughly combined. Transfer the mixture to a floured cutting board and roll into ¼-inch thick ropes. Cut into small pieces about 1-inch long.

Bring a large pot of salted water to a boil and add the gnocchi. Once the water returns to a boil, let them cook for just a few minutes and then drain. Toss with melted butter and serve sprinkled with Parmesan.

Cook's tip Add sage leaves to the melted butter for extra flavor.

Cavatelli with Zucchini and Mushrooms

Serves 4

2 medium zucchini, with flowers attached
3 tablespoons extra-virgin olive oil
1 shallot, minced
salt and freshly ground pepper
3½ ounces mixed wild mushrooms in oil, drained
2 parsley sprigs, minced
1 pinch dried saffron
11 ounces fresh cavatelli or orecchiette
2 tablespoons grated Parmesan cheese

Preparation time 15 minutes
Cooking time 15 minutes
Level easy

Detach the zucchini flowers and thinly slice. Cut the zucchini in half lengthwise and then slice each half into half-moons.

Heat the olive oil in a frying pan and add the shallot. Add a little water and simmer until soft. Add the zucchini and season with salt. Sauté over high heat for a few minutes. Add ½ cup water, cover, and cook for 5 minutes. Add the mushrooms, parsley, saffron, and zucchini blossoms. Cook for 2 to 3 minutes.

Cook the cavatelli in a large pot of salted boiling water until al dente. Drain, reserving a little cooking water, and transfer the cavatelli and cooking water to the pan with the zucchini. Sprinkle with Parmesan cheese and season with freshly ground pepper. Drizzle with olive oil and sauté for 2 minutes. Serve immediately.

Variation Try making cavatelli with arugula. Sauté minced onion, carrot, and celery with 1 garlic clove and a few basil leaves. Add 2 cups (10½ ounces) cherry tomatoes and cook for 20 minutes. Cook 14 ounces cavatelli in salted boiling water; a few minutes before draining the pasta, add 2 bunches of chopped arugula, to the pot. Drain the pasta and arugula and add to the tomatoes. Toss to coat. Drizzle with olive oil and top with chili pepper flakes and grated pecorino cheese.

Asparagus and Smoked Scamorza Lasagne

Serves 4

2 ¼ pounds asparagus
1 shallot, minced
1 ladleful vegetable broth
½ cup (1 stick) butter
½ cup (2 ounces) all-purpose flour
3 cups hot milk
salt and pepper
½ package (8 ounces) lasagne noodles
3 ½ ounces smoked scamorza cheese or smoked mozzarella, grated
1 cup (3 ½ ounces) grated Parmesan cheese

Preparation time 30 minutes
Cooking time 20 minutes
Level easy

Preheat the oven to 350°F.

Slice the asparagus stems into rounds and leave the tips intact. Blanch the tips for 3 to 4 minutes in salted boiling water.

Cook the shallot in a saucepan with a little water until soft. Add the asparagus stems and cook for a few minutes. Add the vegetable broth and cook for 10 minutes. Remove from heat and puree.

Meanwhile, melt half the butter over low heat. Stir in the flour and cook for a few minutes. Slowly whisk in the hot milk. Cook stirring constantly, until thick. Add the asparagus puree and season with salt and pepper.

Cook the lasagne noodles in a large pot of salted boiling water for 1 minute. Drain with a slotted spoon and place on a clean kitchen towel to dry.

Butter an 8-inch square baking dish and place a sheet or two of lasagne in the bottom of the dish. Top with a ladleful of sauce and sprinkle with scamorza and Parmesan. Place one-third of the asparagus tips on top of the cheese and cover with another sheet of pasta. Continue making layers until the ingredients are finished. Brush the final layer of pasta with the remaining melted butter and sprinkle with Parmesan cheese. Bake for 15 minutes. Serve immediately.

Rice, Zucchini, and Egg Timbales

Serves 4

1 ¼ cups (9 ounces) parboiled rice
salt and pepper
3 tablespoons extra-virgin olive oil
1 garlic clove, smashed
3 firm zucchini, julienned
4 eggs
1 tablespoon grated Parmesan

Preparation time 25 minutes
Cooking time 30 minutes
Level easy

Boil the rice in salted water until al dente and drain. Rinse the rice under cold running water.

Heat the olive oil in a nonstick frying pan and sauté the garlic clove. Add the zucchini and sauté briefly, about 2 minutes. Season to taste with salt and pepper. Stir the zucchini into the rice.

Beat the eggs with the Parmesan and pinches of salt and pepper. Pour a ladleful of the egg mixture into a hot nonstick frying pan to form a thin omelet, then remove from the pan. Continue making omelets until the egg mixture is gone. Using a cookie cutter, cut the omelets into rounds.

In 4 small ramekins, make layers of the rice mixture and the omelet rounds until all of the ingredients have been used up. Press down to compact, then invert them onto serving plates. Drizzle with olive oil and top with a few marjoram leaves, if desired.

Variation For extra flavor, sprinkle a little curry powder in the ramekins before filling them.

Spaetzle with Caponata

1

2

3

Serves 4

Spaetzle
2 cups (9 ounces) all-purpose flour
½ cup milk
2 eggs
salt and pepper
ground nutmeg
extra-virgin olive oil

Caponata
1 zucchini
½ yellow bell pepper
2 vine-ripened tomatoes
3 tablespoons extra-virgin olive oil
2 tablespoons pine nuts
salt
4 tablespoons pitted black olives, chopped
2 tablespoons capers, rinsed and dried
3 basil leaves
dried red chili pepper flakes

Preparation time 30 minutes
Cooking time 12 minutes
Level easy

Mix the flour in a bowl with the milk and eggs. Whisk to form a smooth, thick batter. Season with salt, pepper, and nutmeg.

Bring a large pot of water to a boil, then add salt. Pour the batter into a spaetzle grater or form tiny dumplings with a spoon, and drop directly into the boiling water (photo 1). Cook the spaetzle for 3 to 4 minutes, drain, and rinse in cold water. Drizzle with a little olive oil.

Dice the zucchini (photo 2) and bell pepper (photo 3) and blanch for 2 minutes in salted boiling water. Blanch the tomatoes, then drain, peel, seed, and chop. Heat the olive oil in a frying pan and add the pine nuts. Toast briefly and then add the peppers, zucchini, and tomatoes. Season with salt and add the olives, capers, and basil.

Transfer the spaetzle into the pan with the caponata and sauté over high heat for a few minutes. Sprinkle with chili pepper flakes and serve.

Alternatively, serve the spaetzle over the caponata.

Linguine with Mint Pesto

Serves 4

5 tablespoons extra-virgin olive oil
1 spring onion, sliced
2 cups (10½ ounces) green cherry tomatoes, quartered
1 bunch of mint plus extra for garnish
½ garlic clove
¼ cup (1 ounce) almonds, chopped
4 tablespoons grated Parmesan cheese
11 ounces linguine
4 ounces aged pecorino Sardo cheese, shaved

Preparation time 10 minutes
Cooking time 15 minutes
Level easy

Heat 2 tablespoons of the olive oil in a large frying pan. Add the spring onion and sauté for a few minutes. Add the tomatoes and sauté over high heat for 5 minutes.

Blend the mint leaves and garlic with the remaining olive oil in a food processor or with a mortar and pestle. Add the almonds, Parmesan, and a little cold water. Blend until the pesto is smooth.

Cook the pasta in a large pot of salted boiling water until al dente. Drain and transfer the pasta to the pan with the tomatoes. Add the mint pesto and the shaved pecorino. Mix, then garnish with mint leaves. Serve immediately.

Fusilli with Potatoes, Cannellini Beans, and Mint

Serves 4

½ cup (3½ ounces) dried cannellini beans or other white beans
1 bay leaf
1 medium potato
3 tablespoons extra-virgin olive oil
2 shallots, minced
salt
1 dried red chili pepper
11 ounces fusilli
6 mint leaves, julienned

Preparation time 15 minutes
Cooking time 35 minutes
Level easy

Soak the beans overnight, then boil them with the bay leaf until tender.

Peel and dice the potato, then soak it in cold water. Set aside.

Heat the oil in a frying pan and add the shallots, a pinch of salt, and a little water. Sauté until the shallots are soft. Add the beans along with a little of their cooking water and the drained potato. Crumble in the chili pepper and cover. Cook for 20 minutes over medium heat, adding water if the sauce becomes too dry.

Cook the fusilli in a large pot of salted water until al dente. Drain, transfer to the sauce, and toss to coat. Garnish with mint leaves and serve.

Cook's tip This dish makes a nutritionally complete meal. The mint leaves give the pasta a particular flavor, but may be substituted with other herbs such as basil, marjoram, parsley, or dill. Add pecorino or Parmesan cheese to enhance the flavor even further.

Cornmeal Tagliatelle with Radicchio and Provolone

Serves 4

1¼ cups (5 ounces) all-purpose flour
1 cup (5 ounces) finely ground cornmeal
salt and pepper
3 eggs
2 tablespoons semolina flour
2 tablespoons extra-virgin olive oil
1 shallot, minced
1 head Treviso radicchio or other radicchio, sliced
½ cup (2 ounces) walnuts, chopped
3½ ounces provolone, diced

Preparation time 30 minutes
Cooking time 10 minutes
Level easy

Mix the flour and cornmeal with a pinch of salt in a bowl and add the eggs. Mix with your fingers to combine. Transfer the dough to a floured work surface and knead with the palm of your hand until smooth. Cover with plastic wrap and refrigerate for 30 minutes.

Roll out the dough into thin sheets using a pasta machine. Fold each sheet into quarters and slice into thin tagliatelle (about the width of fettuccine), or cut tagliatelle with the pasta machine's attachment. Spread the tagliatelle on a wooden board and sprinkle with the semolina flour.

Heat the olive oil in a nonstick frying pan and add the minced shallot. Let soften, then add the radicchio and the walnuts. Sprinkle with a little water, season with salt and pepper, and add the provolone.

Cook the pasta in a large pot of salted boiling water for 2 minutes. Drain and transfer to the sauce. Toss to coat. Serve immediately.

Eggplant and Polenta Lasagne

Serves 4 to 6

sunflower oil, for frying
1 large eggplant, thinly sliced
3 tablespoons extra-virgin olive oil
2 garlic cloves, peeled and smashed
1 cup (6 ounces) canned crushed tomatoes
basil, torn into small pieces
salt and pepper
1 cup plus 2 tablespoons (6 ounces) instant cornmeal polenta
9 ounces mozzarella, diced
3 tablespoons grated Parmesan cheese

Preparation time 20 minutes
Cooking time 35 minutes
Level easy

Preheat the oven to 375°F.

Heat sunflower oil in a frying pan and fry the eggplant slices. Drain with a slotted spoon or tongs and lay on paper towels to dry.

Heat the olive oil in a saucepan, add the garlic, and sauté until the cloves begin to change color. Add the crushed tomatoes and let simmer for 10 minutes. Add the basil and season with salt and pepper to taste.

Bring the water to a boil in a saucepan with a little salt. Whisk in the polenta and stir with a wooden spoon until the polenta is still quite soft, but not liquid. Add the polenta to the tomato sauce and mix well.

In a well-oiled baking dish make layers of eggplant, tomato-polenta mixture, and mozzarella, finishing with a layer of eggplant topped with the remaining mozzarella. Sprinkle with Parmesan and bake for 15 minutes. Remove from the oven, cut into squares, and serve.

Cook's tip For a lighter version of this variation on the traditional eggplant alla parmigiana, try grilling the eggplant in a cast-iron grill pan instead of frying.

Warm Farro and Artichoke Salad

Serves 4

1 ¼ cups (9 ounces) pearled farro or barley
salt
1 tablespoon extra-virgin olive oil
1 shallot, minced
4 baby artichokes, trimmed and thinly sliced
1 pinch saffron
1 bunch puntarelle, frisée, or endive, chopped

Preparation time 15 minutes
Cooking time 55 minutes
Level easy

Cook the farro or barley in boiling salted water for 30 minutes. Drain and let sit for 20 minutes.

Heat the olive oil in a frying pan and sauté the shallot until soft. Add the artichokes and the saffron and cook for 20 minutes. Add the puntarelle, frisee, or endive and sauté for a few more minutes. Add the cooked farro or barley, sauté another 5 minutes, then serve.

Variation Here's another idea for a tasty farro salad. Boil the farro in salted water until tender. Drain and let sit for 30 minutes. Meanwhile infuse extra-virgin olive oil with garlic and chili pepper, then strain. Toss the farro with the garlic-chili oil and 10 shredded basil leaves. Julienne 2 carrots, 2 zucchini, and 2 celery stalks and add to the farro together with 2 handfuls of olives. Serve chilled.

Mezze Maniche with Celery-Leaf Pesto

Serves 4

Pasta
1 pound celery leaves
6 basil leaves
1 sprig of wild fennel or dill
4 to 5 mint leaves
2/3 cup (3½ ounces) almonds, toasted
5 tablespoons grated Parmesan cheese
1 garlic clove
8 tablespoons extra-virgin olive oil
salt
13 ounces mezze maniche (or rigatoni)

Garnish
mixed herbs, minced
sliced almonds

Preparation time 20 minutes
Cooking time 15 minutes
Level easy

Blend the celery leaves, basil, wild fennel or dill, mint, almonds, Parmesan, garlic, and 6 tablespoons extra-virgin olive oil in a food processor until smooth.

Bring a large pot of salted water to a boil and cook the pasta until al dente. Drain and sauté in a frying pan with the remaining 2 tablespoons olive oil. Transfer to a bowl and toss with the pesto. Garnish with minced herbs and sliced almonds.

Variation The almonds can be replaced with the same quantity of pine nuts, or the celery leaves replaced with fennel leaves or dill.

Beyond Meat

Unusual ingredients form creative
vegetarian main courses,
featuring natural alternatives
to meat and fish as the base
for tasty and healthy meals.

Grilled Tofu with Sautéed Vegetables

Serves 4, as a side dish

2 tablespoons extra-virgin olive oil
1 garlic clove
1 celery stalk, diced
1 carrot, diced
½ cup vegetable broth
1 block of extra-firm tofu (10 ounces), sliced
20 spinach leaves, chopped
juice of ½ lemon
salt and pepper

Preparation time 20 minutes
Cooking time 10 minutes
Level easy

Heat the olive oil in a saucepan and add the garlic clove. Sauté until the garlic is soft. Remove the garlic and add the celery and carrot. Cook for 3 minutes, then add the vegetable broth. Reduce heat and cook for another 5 minutes.

Add the spinach and lemon juice to the vegetable mixture and season with salt and pepper. Let sit for a few minutes.

Grill the tofu slices on a cast-iron grill pan. Serve the tofu slices topped with the sautéed vegetables.

Ginger-Lemon Seitan with Olives

Serves 4

2 tablespoons corn oil
1 medium onion, sliced
salt
1 (1-inch) piece fresh ginger root, peeled and minced
14 ounces seitan, sliced into 1-inch strips
juice and julienned zest of 1 lemon
2 tablespoons soy sauce
½ teaspoon kudzu root starch
⅓ cup (2 ounces) pitted black olives
1 bunch of parsley, minced

Preparation time 15 minutes
Cooking time 15 minutes
Level easy

Heat the corn oil in a frying pan and add the onion and a pinch of salt. Let cook until soft. Add the ginger and cook for a few minutes, then add the seitan.

Mix together the lemon juice, soy sauce, and lemon zest. Pour the mixture over the seitan. Cover and cook for 10 to 12 minutes.

Dissolve the kudzu root starch in ½ cup cold water and pour over the seitan. Cook for a few more minutes until the sauce begins to thicken. Add the olives and sprinkle with parsley.

Tempeh with Red Onions and Savoy Cabbage

Serves 4

Tempeh
3 tablespoons extra-virgin olive oil
9 ounces tempeh, thinly sliced
2 red onions, thinly sliced
¼ savoy cabbage, shredded
1 teaspoon soy sauce
vegetable broth
1 teaspoon tahini

Garnish
4 savoy cabbage leaves, blanched

Preparation time 15 minutes
Cooking time 20 minutes
Level easy

Heat 1 tablespoon of the olive oil in a nonstick frying pan and add the tempeh. Sauté briefly. Heat the remaining olive oil in a saucepan and add the onions. Cook for 5 minutes, until soft. Add the cabbage and stir.

Add the soy sauce and let cook for 10 minutes. Add the sautéed tempeh and a little hot broth. Reduce heat and cook for 10 minutes. Add the tahini to thicken the sauce and cook for another 5 minutes. Serve each portion on a blanched cabbage leaf.

Seitan-Stuffed Cabbage

Serves 4

3 tablespoons extra-virgin olive oil
2 shallots, minced
¾ cup vegetable broth
1 bunch black kale, roughly chopped
½ chili pepper, minced
7 ounces seitan, finely diced
2 slices buckwheat sourdough bread, diced
1 savoy cabbage

Preparation time 25 minutes
Cooking time 45 minutes
Level medium

Preheat the oven to 375°F.

Heat the olive oil in a wide pan. Add the shallots and 1 tablespoon of the broth and cook for 2 minutes. Add the kale, chili pepper, and seitan. Cover with the remaining broth and cook for 10 minutes. Remove from heat and add the bread. Mix well so that the bread absorbs all of the cooking liquid.

Remove the tough outer leaves of the savoy cabbage. Cut out the stem and inner core of the cabbage, leaving a 1-inch thick shell. Steam the cabbage for about 15 minutes, or until al dente.

Stuff the cabbage shell with the seitan filling and place in a baking dish. Bake in the lower part of the oven for 20 minutes. Let sit for 20 minutes before serving.

Variation This filling can be used to make a savory strudel. Roll out puff pastry or phyllo dough and top with the seitan filling. Roll up the strudel and bake for 30 minutes at 350°F. Slice and serve.

Green Soybeans with Pine Nuts and Raisins

Serves 4

½ cup (5 ounces) green soybeans
salt
4 bay leaves
2 tablespoons raisins
½ cup Marsala wine
2 tablespoons extra-virgin olive oil
1 white onion, thinly sliced
1 tablespoon pine nuts

Preparation time 20 minutes
Cooking time 50 minutes
Level easy

SOY

One of the most widely used plants in the world, soy is grown for its seeds and shoots, and also harvested to make a wide variety of foods (oil, flour, milk, and other derivatives). Green soy, harvested before the soy is mature, is packed with vegetable proteins and makes an excellent base for soups, stews, and side dishes.

Place the green soybeans in boiling water, salt, and add 2 of the bay leaves. Boil for 50 minutes.

Soak the raisins in the Marsala wine for 5 minutes. Drain the raisins, reserving the wine.

Heat the olive oil in a frying pan and add the onion. Sauté until soft. Add the pine nuts, raisins, and remaining bay leaves. Add the reserved Marsala and reduce. Carefully mix in the drained soybeans.

Place four round cookie cutters on plates and fill with the soy mixture. Remove the cookie cutters and serve immediately.

Variation Make a green soy pâté by thinly slicing 1 large leek and sautéing with 1 teaspoon of soy sauce for 15 minutes. Puree the leek and cooked green soybeans with 2 tablespoons of sesame oil. Spread the pâté on toast, and garnish with minced parsley.

Breaded Seitan with Herbs

Serves 4

3 tablespoons all-purpose flour
1 bunch mixed herbs (parsley, rosemary, thyme, chives), minced
1½ cups (5½ ounces) breadcrumbs
14 ounces seitan, thinly sliced
2 tablespoons extra-virgin olive oil
salt

Preparation time 30 minutes
Cooking time 15 minutes
Level easy

Mix the flour with enough water to form a thin batter.

Separately, mix the herbs with the breadcrumbs. Dip the seitan slices in the batter, then coat with the herbed breadcrumbs. Press down with your hands to make sure the breadcrumbs adhere.

Heat the olive oil in a frying pan and fry the seitan until golden brown on both sides. Remove from the pan and drain on paper towels. Season with salt and serve immediately.

Spicy Seitan

Serves 4

extra-virgin olive oil
1 garlic clove
1 chili pepper
2 rosemary sprigs
1 package (8 ounces) seitan, chopped
½ cup white wine
2 tablespoons soy sauce
1 teaspoon kudzu root starch

Preparation time 10 minutes
Cooking time 20 minutes
Level easy

Heat olive oil in a frying pan and add the garlic, chili pepper, and rosemary. Add the seitan and sauté briefly. Add the wine wine and let cook for 20 minutes. Transfer the seitan to a serving plate and drizzle with soy sauce.

Dissolve the kudzu root starch in 2 tablespoons water. Add the mixture to the pan juices and cook until thick. Pour the sauce over the seitan and serve immediately.

Tofu, Seitan, and Vegetable Skewers

Serves 4

2 zucchini
2 carrots
1 red bell pepper
salt
1 bunch radishes, trimmed
10½ ounces seitan, cubed
9 ounces tofu, cubed
3 tablespoons soy sauce
1 bunch mixed herbs (rosemary, thyme, marjoram, chives), minced
2 garlic cloves, smashed
1 tablespoon kudzu root starch

Preparation time 30 minutes
Cooking time 10 minutes
Level easy

Chop the zucchini, carrots, and bell pepper into equal-size pieces. Blanch the vegetable pieces separately in lightly salted water. Blanch the whole radishes. Thread the vegetables, seitan, and tofu onto skewers.

Mix together the soy sauce, 3 tablespoons water, the herbs, and the garlic cloves. Marinate the skewers in this mixture for at least 2 hours.

Sear the skewers in a nonstick frying pan over high heat for 3 to 4 minutes per side.

Dissolve the kudzu in a little salted water. Drizzle over the skewers and cook for 1 more minute.

Potato and Nut Patties

Serves 4

2 small yellow-fleshed potatoes (about 10½ ounces)
salt and pepper
1 tablespoon shelled pistachios, roughly chopped, plus extra for garnish
1 tablespoon pine nuts, roughly chopped
2 tablespoons walnuts, roughly chopped, plus extra for garnish
1 egg
3 tablespoons breadcrumbs
2 tablespoons extra-virgin olive oil
sage leaves

Preparation time 20 minutes
Cooking time 40 minutes
Level easy

Boil the potatoes in salted water until tender. Drain. As soon as they cool slightly, peel and mash them. Add the pistachios, pine nuts, walnuts, egg, and 1 tablespoon breadcrumbs. Season with salt and pepper and mix together.

Form the mixture into patties by shaping them inside a cookie cutter, smoothing the top with the back of a spoon. Dip them in the remaining breadcrumbs.

Heat the oil with the sage in a nonstick frying pan and cook the patties for 2 minutes on each side. Serve hot, garnished with extra walnuts and pistachios.

Vegetables

Bring delicious and healthy
dishes to the table with light
and colorful vegetables
prepared simply in original ways.

Steamed Spinach with Sweet and Sour Onions

Serves 4

1 tablespoon raisins
¼ cup Vin Santo or other sweet dessert wine
4 tablespoons (2 ounces) butter
2 yellow onions, thinly sliced
1 tablespoon pine nuts
salt and pepper
1 teaspoon white wine vinegar
18 ounces spinach leaves

Preparation time 15 minutes
Cooking time 10 minutes
Level easy

Soak the raisins in the Vin Santo with a little warm water. Drain and set aside.

Heat the butter in a frying pan. Add the onions and cook over low heat until they begin to soften. Add the pine nuts and raisins. Pour over the vinegar and let it evaporate. Add a few spoonfuls of water and season with salt and pepper. Cook, uncovered, until the water has evaporated.

Meanwhile, steam the spinach. Squeeze out the excess water. Place four round cookie cutters on serving plates. Fill the cookie cutters with the steamed spinach, top with the sweet and sour onions, and remove the cookie cutters. Serve immediately.

Note When browning or sautéing ingredients, adding a liquid (usually alcohol or broth) and letting it evaporate helps slow down the cooking and also adds extra flavor.

Swiss Chard and Cannellini Rolls

Serves 4

5 tablespoons extra-virgin olive oil
1 onion, minced
salt
2 carrots, sliced
1 cup cooked cannellini beans
12 medium-size Swiss chard leaves
1 garlic clove, sliced

Preparation time 15 minutes
Cooking time 30 minutes
Level easy

Preheat the oven to 350°F.

Heat 2 tablespoons olive oil in a large saucepan and add the onion and a pinch of salt. Let soften and add the carrots and another pinch of salt.

Sauté over high heat for a few minutes. Add the beans and a little water. Cook for 10 minutes and puree the mixture in a food processor. The mixture should be soft but not liquid. Season with salt to taste.

Blanch the Swiss chard leaves in boiling water for 3 minutes. Drain and dry on a clean kitchen towel. Spread the Swiss chard out on a work surface and fill each leaf with 1 tablespoon of the bean-carrot puree. Fold in the sides of the leaf and roll up.

Place the rolls in an oiled baking dish and add the sliced garlic along with 2 to 3 tablespoons of water. Bake for 10 minutes and serve immediately.

Cook's tip Beans are an important source of vegetable protein, and can play a vital role in a vegetarian or vegan diet. They are rich in complex carbohydrates, B vitamins such as folic acid, and minerals such as iron and potassium. Moreover, they are low in fat and high in fiber.

Swiss Chard Rolls with Tofu and Pumpkin

Serves 4

8 Swiss chard leaves
4 tablespoons extra-virgin olive oil
1 garlic clove
2 cups (9 ounces) chopped pumpkin
  or other winter squash
7 ounces tofu, diced
1 tablespoon soy sauce
1 thyme sprig

Preparation time 15 minutes
Cooking time 20 minutes
Level easy

TOFU
Tofu should be refrigerated and may be kept in water for up to 3 days after opening. An easily digestible food, it is neutral in taste and thus pairs well with many flavors.

Blanch the Swiss chard leaves in boiling water for a few minutes. Drain and spread out on a clean kitchen towel.

Heat 2 tablespoons olive oil and the garlic in a frying pan. When the garlic begins to brown, remove it and add the pumpkin; cook for 5 minutes. Add the tofu and 2 tablespoons water and cook until the pumpkin is tender. Add the soy sauce, remove from the heat, and let sit for 10 minutes.

Place the tofu mixture on the Swiss chard leaves. Fold in the sides of each leaf and roll up. Secure the rolls with toothpicks. Sauté the rolls in 2 tablespoons olive oil for a few minutes. Garnish with thyme leaves and serve immediately.

Cauliflower and Broccoli with Mustard-Miso Sauce

Serves 4

Vegetables
1 small cauliflower (about 7 ounces), cut into florets
1 head broccoli (about 9 ounces), cut into florets
salt
extra-virgin olive oil

Sauce
1 garlic clove
1 teaspoon barley miso
½ teaspoon mustard
1 tablespoon ginger juice
2 tablespoons lemon juice
1 teaspoon malted rice powder
2 tablespoons sesame oil
salt

Preparation time 20 minutes
Cooking time 10 minutes
Level easy

Steam the broccoli and cauliflower florets with a pinch of salt. Remove from the steamer when tender and reserve the cooking water.

Smash the garlic clove in a suribachi (or with a mortar and pestle) and mix with the remaining sauce ingredients along with 1 to 2 tablespoons of the reserved cooking water.

Sauté the broccoli and cauliflower in a little olive oil for a few minutes, then serve with the sauce.

Barley Parcels with Tofu and Artichokes

Serves 4

Filling
4 small artichokes
juice of 1 lemon
3 tablespoons extra-virgin olive oil
1 garlic clove
white wine (optional)
7 ounces chopped tofu
salt
parsley, chopped

Dough
1 cup (5 ounces) barley flour
½ cup (2 ounces) whole-wheat flour
½ cup (2 ounces) all-purpose flour
4 tablespoons extra-virgin olive oil
salt

Preparation time 40 minutes
Cooking time 30 minutes
Level easy

Preheat the oven to 325°F.

Trim the artichokes, removing all of the tough outer leaves and discarding the inner choke from each. Thinly slice the artichokes and place in a bowl of cold water and lemon juice.

Heat the oil for the filling and the garlic in a frying pan and add the drained artichokes. Add a little white wine if desired. After 10 minutes, add the tofu and a pinch of salt and continue cooking until the artichokes are tender. Add the parsley.

Meanwhile, mix the three flours with the olive oil, salt, and enough boiling water to form a smooth and elastic dough. Roll out the dough and cut into squares. Place a spoonful of artichoke filling on each square and fold in the corners to make a little package. Brush the squares with oil and bake for 20 minutes. Serve warm.

Variation The barley parcels can also be filled with a seasonal vegetable and tofu ragù. For another variation, try making mini-strudels instead of squares by rolling the dough around the filling, then making incisions on the top. Cook as indicated in the recipe above.

Chickpea-Stuffed Fennel with Sesame Seeds

Serves 4

1 cup (7 ounces) dried chickpeas, soaked overnight
1 bay leaf
2 garlic cloves
1 tablespoon tahini
salt and pepper
6 round fennel bulbs, halved, green leaves reserved
4 tablespoons extra-virgin olive oil
1 thyme sprig
2 tablespoons sesame seeds

Preparation time 35 minutes
Cooking time 2 hours
Level easy

Preheat the oven to 350°F.

Boil the chickpeas with the bay leaf and 1 garlic clove for at least 50 minutes, until the chickpeas are tender. Then puree the chickpeas with a little bit of the cooking water in a food processor to obtain a thick cream. Add the tahini and season with salt and pepper.

Blanch the fennel bulb halves, then dry on a clean kitchen towel. Using a spoon, make a cavity in the center of each. Puree the fennel that was removed and add it to the chickpea puree. Fill the fennel halves with the mixture.

Place the stuffed fennel in an oiled baking dish and top with thyme leaves and the reserved green fennel leaves. Add the garlic clove to the dish and drizzle the stuffed fennel with olive oil. Sprinkle with sesame seeds and bake for 10 to 15 minutes. Serve hot or warm.

Roasted Vegetables

Serves 4

1 eggplant, peeled and cubed
3 zucchini, thickly sliced
2 large carrots, thickly sliced
1 white onion, diced
10 cherry tomatoes
salt and pepper
2 tablespoons extra-virgin olive oil

Preparation time 10 minutes
Cooking time 25 minutes
Level easy

Preheat the oven to 400°F.

Mix the eggplant, zucchini, carrots, onion, and tomatoes together and season with salt and pepper. Oil a baking dish, add the vegetables, and drizzle with olive oil.

Bake for 25 minutes, stirring the vegetables a few times. Remove from the oven, cool to room temperature, and serve.

Eggplant Neapolitan

Serves 6

6 eggplants (use a seedless variety), sliced lengthwise
1¾ pounds San Marzano or Roma tomatoes, diced
1 spring onion, chopped
1 bunch of Neapolitan basil
salt and freshly ground black pepper
2 cups extra-virgin olive oil
10 ounces mozzarella, julienned
2 eggs
7 tablespoons grated Parmesan cheese

Preparation time 30 minutes
Cooking time 1 hour 10 minutes
Level easy

Salt the eggplant slices. Place in a colander and let sit for 1 hour. Preheat the oven to 325°F.

Meanwhile, cook the tomatoes, spring onion, and a few basil leaves in a saucepan until softened. Pass the mixture through a food mill and return to heat. Cook for 10 minutes and season with salt and pepper to taste.

Rinse and dry the eggplant slices with paper towels. Heat the olive oil in a frying pan and fry the eggplant slices. When golden, drain the eggplant on paper towels.

Mix together the mozzarella and three-quarters of the remaining basil leaves. Add the eggs to the tomato sauce and stir for a few minutes until well combined.

Spread 3 tablespoons of tomato mixture in a baking dish and top with a layer of eggplant. Sprinkle with 1 tablespoon of the grated Parmesan and some basil. Cover with 2 to 3 tablespoons of sauce and add half the mozzarella. Make a second layer of tomato, eggplant, Parmesan, basil, tomato, and mozzarella. Top with the remaining Parmesan. Bake for 1 hour. Let cool slightly before serving.

Tofu Stir-Fry

Serves 4

2 tablespoons extra-virgin olive oil
1 garlic clove
1 small yellow onion, thinly sliced
2 carrots, sliced
2 zucchini, sliced
1 head broccoli, cut into florets
1 tablespoon sesame seeds
salt
2 small blocks of tofu (18 ounces), chopped
vegetable broth (optional)

Preparation time 20 minutes
Cooking time 25 minutes
Level easy

Heat the olive oil and garlic in a frying pan. When the garlic begins to change color, add the onion. Sauté until soft and add the carrots and zucchini. Cook over medium heat for 5 minutes.

Blanch the broccoli in salted boiling water for 5 minutes. Drain the broccoli and add it to the other vegetables. Sprinkle in the sesame seeds and season with salt to taste.

Add the tofu and a little water or vegetable broth. Cover and cook for 15 minutes. Serve immediately.

Note This dish is also tasty when served at room temperature.

Carrots and Green Beans with Tahini Sauce

TAHINI

Tahini is a paste made from toasted sesame seeds. It is rich in protein, minerals, and unsaturated fats. This versatile seasoning may be used in both sweet and savory foods.

Serves 4

Vegetables
3 cups (12½ ounces) green beans, trimmed
salt
4 carrots, sliced

Sauce
1 pickled, pitted umeboshi plum (or 1 teaspoon umeboshi paste)
1 tablespoon tahini
1 spring onion, sliced
parsley, chopped

Preparation time 25 minutes
Cooking time 10 minutes
Level easy

Blanch the green beans in lightly salted boiling water. After a few minutes, add the carrots to the green beans. When the vegetables are tender but not soft, drain them, reserving a little of the cooking water. Transfer to a bowl.

Mash the umeboshi together with the tahini using a suribachi or mortar and pestle. When the mixture is smooth, dilute it with a little of the reserved cooking water.

Top the vegetables with the sliced spring onion, tahini sauce, and chopped parsley. Mix and serve immediately.

Note Umeboshi are pickled ume fruit, often called plums but more similar to apricots. Umeboshi are preserved in salt and aged in wooden barrels for more than a year. Whole umeboshi, umeboshi paste, and umeboshi vinegar are available at specialty stores and can be used to replace salt or vinegar.

Fennel and Leek Gratin

Serves 4

Vegetables
2 fennel bulbs, quartered
2 leeks, sliced lengthwise

Béchamel
2 tablespoons sesame oil
2 tablespoons rice flour
1 cup soy milk
salt
2 tablespoons white miso

Garnish
1 tablespoon sliced almonds

Preparation time 20 minutes
Cooking time 20 minutes
Level easy

Preheat the oven to 400°F.

Blanch the fennel and the leeks and place them in a baking dish.

Heat the sesame oil in a saucepan and add the flour. Cook the flour for a few minutes over low heat and then whisk in the soy milk, stirring constantly. Cook over low heat for 7 to 8 minutes and season with salt. Stir in the miso and pour the béchamel over the vegetables.

Top with the sliced almonds and bake. After 5 minutes, switch the oven to the broil setting and broil until golden brown.

Tofu and Shiitake Rolls

Serves 4

4 dried shiitake mushrooms, stemmed
2 tablespoons extra-virgin olive oil
1 shallot, minced
2 tablespoons vegetable broth
1 block of tofu (10 ounces), diced
1 tablespoon dried thyme leaves
4 savoy cabbage leaves
1 teaspoon gomasio (see note p. 42)

Preparation time 20 minutes
Cooking time 40 minutes
Level easy

Soak the mushrooms in water for 2 hours. Preheat the oven to 350°F.

Heat the olive oil in a frying pan and sauté the minced shallot. Add the vegetable broth, then the tofu, and cook for 5 minutes. Add the thyme leaves.

Drain and thinly slice the mushrooms, then sauté for a few minutes in a separate frying pan. Add them to the tofu mixture.

Blanch the cabbage leaves and dry them on a clean kitchen towel. Place a few tablespoons of the tofu-mushroom mixture on each leaf. Fold in the sides and roll up the leaves, securing with toothpicks if necessary. Sprinkle with gomasio and bake for 15 minutes.

Cook's tip The shiitake are a kind of Japanese mushroom traditionally used for medicinal purposes. Thought to be a cure for common colds, heart problems, and hypertension, these mushrooms were also used to combat problems linked to high cholesterol. Interestingly, cooking shiitake mushrooms doesn't destroy these important properties but enhances them. Soak the dried mushrooms in 1 cup of water and cover with a plate so they remain immersed. The soaking liquid makes an excellent broth or base for soups.

Leek Gratin with Béchamel

Serves 4

Leeks
4 short fat leeks, trimmed
salt
1 tablespoon sesame oil
½ cup (2 ounces) breadcrumbs

Béchamel
2 tablespoons corn oil
⅓ cup plus 2 tablespoons (2 ounces) all-purpose flour
1¾ cups soy milk
salt
ground nutmeg

Preparation time 10 minutes
Cooking time 45 minutes
Level easy

Preheat the oven to 350°F.

Blanch the leeks in salted boiling water for 7 to 8 minutes. Drain and slice lengthwise. Coat a baking dish with sesame oil and add the leeks. Top with a few tablespoons of breadcrumbs.

Heat the corn oil in a saucepan and add the flour. Cook for a few minutes over low heat. Slowly whisk in the soy milk. Cook over low heat, stirring constantly for 15 minutes. Season with salt and ground nutmeg.

Pour the béchamel over the leeks and sprinkle the remaining breadcrumbs over the top. Bake for 15 to 20 minutes. Serve immediately.

Baked Stuffed Artichokes

Serves 4

Artichokes
12 medium artichokes
1 lemon
salt
1 egg
breadcrumbs
extra-virgin olive oil

Filling
3 ½ ounces ricotta cheese
3 ounces pecorino cheese, grated
1 egg yolk
salt and pepper

Preparation time 30 minutes
Cooking time 15 minutes
Level easy

Preheat the oven to 375°F.

Trim the artichokes, removing the hard outer leaves (photo 1). Rub a cut lemon over the artichokes (photo 2). Cook the artichokes in salted boiling water until just tender. Drain and dry on a clean kitchen towel. Remove the inner choke from each with a paring knife.

Mix together the ricotta, pecorino, and egg yolk. Season with salt and pepper.

Stuff the center of the artichoke with the cheese filling (photo 3). Beat the egg. Dip the top of the stuffed artichokes in the egg and then dip in breadcrumbs. Place the artichokes in an oiled baking dish and bake for 10 minutes. The artichokes may be served hot, at room temperature, or cold.

Turnip Gratin

Serves 4

4 white turnips, peeled and thinly sliced
1 tablespoon umeboshi vinegar (or red wine vinegar, although it's not as salty)
2 tablespoons extra-virgin olive oil
¾ cup (3 ounces) pistachios, chopped
3 tablespoons soy cream
salt and pepper

Preparation time 30 minutes
Cooking time 30 minutes
Level easy

Preheat the oven to 400°F.

Blanch the turnip slices in water with the umeboshi vinegar. Line a baking dish with parchment paper. Coat the paper with olive oil, then cover with a layer of turnips, followed by a layer consisting of some of the pistachios mixed with 1 tablespoon of the soy cream. Continue alternating layers in this manner until the turnips are finished, and top with a with a layer of soy cream and pistachios. Bake for 25 minutes.

Note Turnips are a traditional peasant food in Europe, particularly in the north. The root of the turnip is white and crunchy with an intense flavor. Turnips should be harvested just before maturity while they are still firm but not too hard. The tender inner leaves of the turnip plant are also tasty, as well as full of vitamins.

Asparagus Puree with Jerusalem Artichokes

Serves 4

3 tablespoons extra-virgin olive oil
1 shallot, minced
1 small potato, diced
6 asparagus spears, peeled and sliced
2 cups vegetable broth
salt and pepper
2 Jerusalem artichokes, peeled and diced
2 tablespoons soy sauce

Preparation time 15 minutes
Cooking time 20 minutes
Level easy

Heat 2 tablespoons of olive oil in a frying pan and sauté the minced shallot until soft. Add the potato and brown for 2 minutes. Add the asparagus and cover with vegetable broth. Simmer for 15 minutes. Puree until creamy with an immersion blender or in a food processor or blender, and season with salt and pepper to taste.

Meanwhile, heat the remaining olive oil in a frying pan and add the Jerusalem artichokes. Sauté for 7 to 8 minutes. Add the soy sauce, toss to coat, and sauté over high heat for another 3 minutes.

Serve the asparagus puree in shallow bowls with the Jerusalem artichokes.

Note The potato in this recipe can be replaced by 2 tablespoons of rice or barley flour. Pureed cooked rice may also be used to thicken soups.

Stuffed Squash Blossoms

Serves 4

Squash blossoms

16 squash blossoms
4 potatoes
4 baby zucchini, diced
1 garlic clove
2 marjoram sprigs
2 eggs
6 tablespoons grated Parmesan
3 tablespoons crumbled aged goat cheese
salt and pepper
2 tablespoons extra-virgin olive oil

Sauce

1 pound cherry tomatoes
6 tablespoons extra-virgin olive oil
2 garlic cloves
6 basil leaves plus extra for garnish
salt and pepper

Preparation time 30 minutes
Cooking time 1 hour
Level medium

Preheat the oven to 350°F.

Wipe the squash blossoms with a damp paper towel and carefully remove the pistils without tearing the flowers. Boil the potatoes for 40 minutes in salted water. Drain, peel, and mash with a fork or potato ricer and let cool.

Puree the zucchini in a food processor with the garlic and marjoram. When the potatoes have cooled, stir in the eggs, grated cheeses, and zucchini mixture and season with salt and pepper.

Open the top part of each squash blossom and fill with the potato mixture. Close the blossom by twisting the top of the flower closed. Place the stuffed blossoms on a baking sheet lined with parchment paper. Drizzle with 2 tablespoons olive oil and bake for 15 minutes.

Meanwhile, cut an X on the top of each tomato with a paring knife. Blanch the tomatoes for 30 seconds in boiling water. Drain, peel, seed, and dice.

Heat 6 tablespoons olive oil in a frying pan and brown the garlic. Add the tomatoes and basil and cook over low heat for 10 minutes. Season with salt and pepper to taste.

Remove the squash blossoms from the oven and transfer to a serving plate. Serve with the tomato sauce and garnish with basil leaves.

Deconstructed Panzanella

Serves 4

1 red bell pepper
1 yellow bell pepper
12 ounces crusty bread, cubed
6 tablespoons extra-virgin olive oil
salt and pepper
2 San Marzano or Roma tomatoes, seeded and diced
2 spring onions, sliced
basil leaves
2 tablespoons balsamic vinegar

Preparation time 20 minutes
Cooking time 15 minutes
Level easy

Roast the peppers over an open flame, under the broiler, or in the oven, then place them in a plastic bag and close. Let the peppers steam for 5 to 10 minutes, then peel, seed, and julienne.

Place the bread cubes on a baking sheet, drizzle with olive oil, and season with salt and pepper. Toast under the broiler for a few minutes.

Mix the tomatoes, spring onions, and basil in a bowl with a pinch of salt, the vinegar, and olive oil.

Line a round cookie or biscuit cutter with the pepper strips. Fill with the bread cubes and tomato mixture. Remove the cookie cutter, season with pepper, and drizzle with olive oil.

Leek and Pumpkin Crêpes with Cheese Sauce

Preparation time 30 minutes
Cooking time 45 minutes
Level medium

Serves 4

Crêpes
3 eggs
1 ½ tablespoons melted butter
2 cups milk
¾ cup plus 1 tablespoon (3 ½ ounces)
  all-purpose flour
½ cup (2 ounces) whole-wheat flour

Filling
1 ½ tablespoons butter
3 leeks: 2 sliced, 1 blanched whole
14 ounces pumpkin, peeled, seeded, and diced
salt and pepper
½ cup vegetable broth
3 tablespoons grated Parmesan
ground nutmeg

Cheese sauce
2 tablespoons butter
4 tablespoons all-purpose flour
1 ¼ cups hot milk
3 ounces mild fontina cheese, diced
salt and pepper
2 tablespoons truffle oil

Preheat the oven to 300°F.

Beat together the eggs, melted butter, and milk (photo 1). Whisk in the two flours to form a liquid batter.

Heat a crêpe pan (or small nonstick frying pan). Pour in 1 small ladleful of batter (photo 2) to evenly coat the pan. Cook for 1 minute, flip, cook for another minute, and remove from pan. Continue making crêpes until the batter is finished.

Sauté the sliced leeks with the butter until soft. Add the pumpkin, a pinch of salt, and the vegetable broth. Let simmer until the pumpkin is very soft. Puree the pumpkin; add the Parmesan and season with salt, pepper, and nutmeg.

Place a spoonful of filling on each crêpe and gather the edges to form a little purse. Tie the crêpe shut with a strip of the blanched leek. Place the filled crêpes in a buttered baking dish and cover with aluminum foil. Bake for 15 minutes.

Melt the butter for the sauce in a saucepan and add the flour. Let toast briefly, stirring frequently. Whisk in the hot milk and cook for 10 minutes. Remove from heat and add the cheese. Add salt, pepper, and the truffle oil. Place 2 tablespoons of the sauce on each serving plate and top with crêpes.

Polenta Squares with Marinated Artichokes

Serves 8

Polenta
pinch of salt
1¼ cups (5 ounces) stone-ground cornmeal
1 tablespoon extra-virgin olive oil

Artichokes
4 to 5 baby artichokes
2 tablespoons extra-virgin olive oil
juice of 1 lemon
salt and pepper

Preparation time 20 minutes
Cooking time 10 minutes
Level easy

Heat 2 cups water with a little salt in a saucepan and whisk in the cornmeal. Cook, stirring constantly, until the polenta is thick and pulls away from the sides of the pan. Dampen a baking dish and pour in the polenta. Smooth with a spatula.

Trim the artichokes, removing the tough outer leaves and the inner choke from each. Thinly slice the artichokes. Whisk 2 tablespoons olive oil with the lemon juice, salt, and pepper to create an emulsion for the artichokes. Pour over the artichokes and let sit for 20 minutes.

Meanwhile, cut the polenta into small squares and sauté them in 1 tablespoon olive oil until browned evenly on all sides. Serve with the artichokes on top.

Savory Strudel with Carrots and Artichokes

Serves 4

Dough
1½ teaspoons dry active yeast
1¼ cups (5 ounces) oat flour
1¼ cups (5 ounces) all-purpose flour
salt
1 tablespoon extra-virgin olive oil

Filling
4 artichokes
juice of 1 lemon
2 tablespoons corn oil
1 shallot, minced
3 carrots, peeled and sliced
salt and pepper
parsley, chopped

Preparation time 30 minutes
Cooking time 50 minutes
Level easy

Dissolve the yeast in ¾ cup warm water. Mix the two flours together, add the yeast mixture, a pinch of salt, and the olive oil. Knead the dough until smooth and elastic. Let rest for an hour in a warm, dry place. Preheat the oven to 375°F.

Trim the artichokes, removing the tough outer leaves and the choke from each. Thinly slice the artichokes and soak in 1 tablespoon water and the lemon juice. Heat the corn oil in a frying pan and add the minced shallot and water. Cook until soft, then add the artichokes and carrots. Let cook for 15 minutes over low heat. Season with salt and pepper and sprinkle with parsley.

Roll out the dough to form a thin sheet. Either place on a baking sheet, top with the filling, and roll up to make one long strudel, or cut the sheet of dough into small squares, top each with a spoonful of filling, and fold the corners inward, pinching closed to make little parcels. Place on a baking sheet. Bake for 35 minutes or until browned.

Vegetable Timbales

EGGS
Eggs are rich in proteins that are more complete than those found in milk products, and more nutritious than those in meat or fish.

Serves 4

3 eggs
2/3 cup low-fat milk
salt and pepper
basil, chopped
1 ¼ cups (5 ounces) peas
10 ½ ounces baby zucchini
  with flowers attached
10 baby carrots
1 ½ tablespoons butter
1 spring onion, thinly sliced

Preparation time 10 minutes
Cooking time 30 minutes
Level easy

Preheat the oven to 400°F.

Beat the eggs with the milk until smooth. Season with salt and pepper and add some chopped basil leaves.

Blanch the peas until al dente. Remove the pistils from the zucchini flowers. Thinly slice the zucchini and flowers. Shave the carrots into ribbons with a potato peeler.

Heat the butter in a frying pan and add the peas, zucchini, carrots, and onion. Sauté briefly and season with salt and pepper.

Butter 4 ramekins and divide the vegetable mixture between them. Add the egg mixture. Bake for 15 to 20 minutes, until firm. Serve warm.

Pea and Spring Onion Puree

Serves 4

3 tablespoons corn oil
1 garlic clove
2 spring onions, thinly sliced, plus extra for garnish
2^2/$_3$ cups (12 ounces) peas
salt
1 cup vegetable broth
chives, chopped

Preparation time 10 minutes
Cooking time 30 minutes
Level easy

Heat the corn oil and garlic in a saucepan. Add the spring onions and sauté until soft. Add the peas, a pinch of salt, and after a few minutes, the vegetable broth. Cover and cook for 25 to 30 minutes over medium heat.

Puree the peas in a food processor or with an immersion blender to obtain a thick cream. Adjust the salt, and garnish with chives and spring onion slices.

Note If the puree seems too thin, add 1 tablespoon cornstarch or kudzu root starch dissolved in a little water, and cook for a few more minutes.

Broccoli Rabe with Fondue Sauce

Serves 2 to 3

10½ ounces broccoli rabe
⅓ cup milk
2 ounces Gruyère cheese, grated
2 ounces Emmenthal cheese, grated
salt
ground cinnamon

Preparation time 25 minutes
Cooking time 15 minutes
Level easy

Steam the broccoli rabe until tender.

Heat the milk in a nonstick saucepan and add the cheeses. Stir until the cheese is completely melted, adding extra milk if necessary.

Place the broccoli rabe on a plate and season with salt. Top with the cheese sauce and sprinkle with ground cinnamon.

Avocado and Grapefruit Salad

Serves 4

1 ripe avocado
2 grapefruits
1 head lettuce, torn into pieces
2 tomatoes, sliced
1 small green bell pepper, seeded and julienned
juice of ½ lemon
½ cup (4½ ounces) plain yogurt
4 tablespoons extra-virgin olive oil
salt and pepper

Preparation time 15 minutes
Level easy

Peel the avocado, halve it, remove the pit, and slice the flesh. Arrange the slices on a serving plate.

Peel the grapefruit and cut it into segments, removing all the white pith and skin. Arrange the segments over the avocado.

Arrange the lettuce in the center of the plate and the tomatoes and green pepper around it. Whisk together the lemon juice, yogurt, oil, salt, and pepper. Serve the salad with the dressing on the side.

Note The salad can be enriched with the addition of toasted nuts like almonds or pine nuts, or croutons of toasted bread.

Glossary

Brown

A quick sautéing of food until it begins to color. Frequently used for onions, shallots, or garlic. Cooking is completed in the oven or on the stovetop over lower heat, usually with added liquid.

Cookie cutters

Made in steel or stainless steel, these kitchen tools come in various shapes and sizes. In Italian cooking, they are known as pasta cutters and are usually round and sometimes fluted. Used to cut out pasta and other types of dough, they can also serve as a mold to shape food when presenting a finished dish.

Farro

Also known as emmer wheat, farro was one of the first domesticated crops. In fact, it was used by the ancient Egyptians to make bread. In recent years it has regained popularity and is now often ground into flour and used to make healthy, delicious, and fiber-rich pastas.

Gomasio

A condiment made from sesame seeds that have been toasted and ground with salt. It is often used instead of salt to season vegetables or salads.

Kudzu

A vine that grows naturally throughout Japan, even in areas with poor soil. The root of the vine is harvested in mountain areas, and starch is extracted from the roots. Kudzu is an important part of Japanese cuisine and traditional medicine. A natural thickening agent, it is used in soups, sauces, desserts, and puddings.

Miso

A traditional Japanese food made by fermenting soy, rice, or barley with salt and a mold culture to produce a thick paste. It is used as a seasoning for sauces and pickles, and particularly as a soup base.

Soy cream

A thick liquid made from soy milk that can be used in place of heavy cream. Soy cream is lactose and cholesterol-free.

Spaetzle

Small dumplings or noodles of German origin, also found in France, Switzerland, and Italy's South Tyrol. Traditionally, spaetzle are made from wheat flour and eggs; however, the variations are endless. The dumplings are boiled briefly and served with melted butter.

Stew

To cook vegetables very slowly over low heat with a little liquid, or only the water left on them after washing, until they become very tender.

Tahini

A creamy sesame seed paste that is frequently used in Asian cooking; it is also served as an appetizer in Greece. Furthermore, it is an essential ingredient in hummus. Sold in jars, tahini may be found in larger supermarkets or specialty stores.

Tempeh

A soy-based protein made by fermenting cooked soybeans. Variations are also made with rice, barley, or wheat. Tempeh is an easily digested protein source that contains important fatty acids such as omega-3. It has a firmer consistency than tofu and is often used in place of meat. Of Indonesian origin, tempeh can be purchased in health food stores or larger supermarkets. Tempeh should be covered with a white cheeselike film, and yellow-colored beans should not be visible.

Tofu

A soy-based protein traditionally used in Chinese and Japanese cuisines. Due to its high nutritional value, it has become an important part of many vegetarian and vegan diets. Tofu is sometimes called "soy cheese" because it looks similar to an unaged cheese and it is made from a process similar to cheese-making.

Index

Printed in China in September 2008